Copyright © 2020 by manulla Rose

All rights reserved. No part of this publication may be reproduced, distributed, or transmitted in any form or by any means, including photocopying, recording, or other electronic or mechanical methods, without the prior written permission of the publisher, except in the case of brief quotations embodied in critical reviews and certain other noncommercial uses permitted by copyright law

A special request Please

A simple review on amazon Really help us out! so if you could take one minut to leave one you are amazing and I love you

This book belongs to :

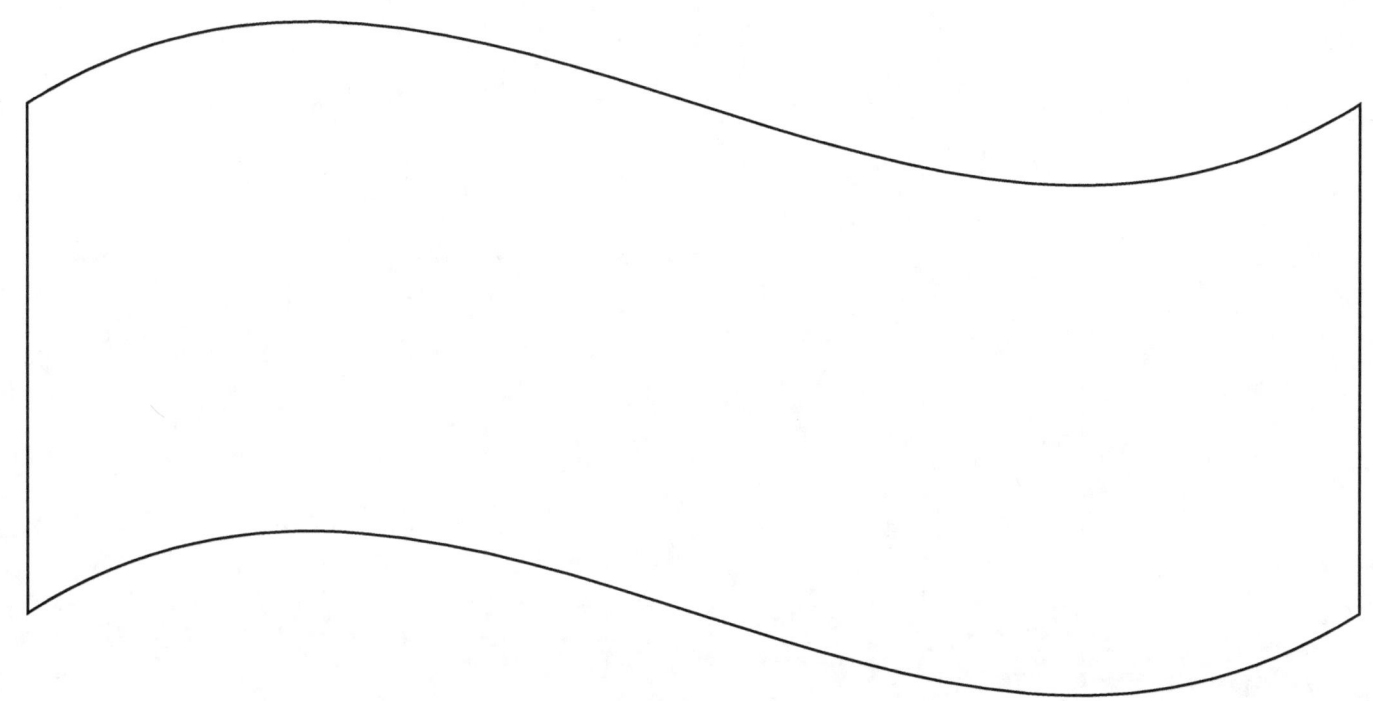

www.ingramcontent.com/pod-product-compliance
Lightning Source LLC
Chambersburg PA
CBHW080953220526
45465CB00008BA/3265